REFLECTIONS

Storte

The Fabric of Light
Kristina Valaitis

REFLECTIONS

Peter Wexler

Photographic images copyright © 2006 Peter Wexler. All rights reserved.

Printed and bound in Hong Kong by C & C Offset Printing Co., Ltd.

Published by U.S. Equities Realty, LLC, Chicago, Illinois.

Designed and typeset by Michael Krzewicki, U.S. Equities Realty.

Principal type faces used in this book are Univers, Meridien and Opsmarckt.

ISBN #978-0-9762914-0-4

For Connie — my wife

Acknowledgements

No one stands alone. I am extremely fortunate to have been associated with lovely, talented, intelligent people all my life. Here are some who have been important in the making of this book – its thoughts, pictures and expressions.

Above the title, Bob Wislow saw the pictures and put his energy, company, taste and sensitivity behind the project. Carrie Berman has thought it through and led us all. Frances Stewart looked at some of my Venice work a few years ago and decided to make it happen – watch out! Christa Kelly and Michael Krzewicki have guided us in pictures and graphics. Holly Birnbaum Sherman minded what we said. And Kristina Valaitis, who was asked by Bob and Carrie to write *something*, created her own wonderful reflections for this book.

These and others are listed here with their companies or, hopefully, by helpful category.

U.S. Equities Realty
Bob Wislow
Carrie Berman
Michael Krzewicki
Tony DiBiase
Peggy Irby

Creative Products International
Frances Todd Stewart
Charlie Stewart
Molly Steffey
Barbara Knolle
Todd Swanson
Cathy Wong

For Peter Wexler
Lap Chi-Chu
Rod Lemmond
Christa Kelly
Hallie Zieselman

New Yorkers
Naomi Warner
Marian Reiner
Marc Zand
Harold Prince

Venetians and Friends
Piera & Franco Agopyan
Sara & Franco Agopyan
Chiara & Francesco Agopyan
Bruno & Alix Battaglia
Daniella Simonata Putz
Daisy & Francesco Savini
Giusi Tamburello

Istituto Venezia
Matteo & Anna Savini

Writing, Editing and Translations
Kristina Valaitis
Holly Birnbaum Sherman
Sergio Stefani
Dott. David Ford

Research
Marlene (Maria-Elena) Putz
Erica Mankowsky

Image Preparation
Testa d'Oro – Venezia
Marco Rigo
Mara Rosso
Digital Ink, New York
Jaime Wollens
Peter Triolo, New York

Exhibition
Lois Weisberg
Greg Knight
Lanny Silverman

Others
Mary & Stephen Klein
Eileen Mackevich

10 *Senza titolo*

Cities of Reflection

I met Peter Wexler four years ago when U.S. Equities was developing the new headquarters for the Compuware Corporation – the pioneer project in downtown Detroit's Campus Martius redevelopment area, which includes the newly created Campus Martius Park. A theatre designer, artist and producer, Peter joined the Campus Martius Park design team to help us create an active community gathering place.

During the course of the project, Peter and I discovered our mutual affinity for Venice. When I visited Peter's New York studio a year later and saw his amazing photographs of Venice, a new door opened in our association. I knew then his unique perspective of Venice deserved a wider audience. For me, his photographs mirror – in a thoroughly original way – the inexplicable experience of being in Venice.

In so many ways, Venice is beyond comparison. It is the only urban center where the primary modes of transportation keep its residents and visitors literally in touch with nature in a way that travelling by bike, car, bus or train cannot. In Venice you must move *on* water in boats large or small, or walk on banks *along* water, on bridges *over* water or even *through* water when the city floods. In the winter, Venetians don their *stivali di gomma* (rubber boots) and put wooden planks on metal sawhorses to create the *passarelle* (raised walkways) that enable them to move through the city during *acqua alta* (high water). After a snowstorm, we Chicagoans put on our galoshes, painstakingly shovel our cars out and then place sawhorses and even kitchen chairs to stake out our parking spots on the streets.

The water itself is an opportunity for pure enjoyment. During the Festival of Redentore, nearly every Venetian takes a boat into the basin to watch the fireworks and have a picnic. This celebration is the forerunner of Chicago's Venetian Night, which includes a twinkling-lighted boat parade on Lake Michigan, musical entertainment and thousands of boats in the harbor watching a fireworks extravaganza. Visitors to Venice can enjoy gliding in a gondola through the quiet back canals, dining at the water's edge and watching the informal regatta every day in the lagoon, composed of boats of every size and type – from flat-bottomed rowboats to small sailboats to the large cruise ships, and everything in between. For most Venetians, however, riding the *vaporetto* (water bus) on the Grand Canal is simply their way of getting to work or going shopping. Clearly, commuting the Venetian way is very appealing. When your only option is to walk or travel slowly by boat, you gain time to think and reflect.

Compared to Venice, Chicago is very young. When the French explorers Joliet and Marquette paddled their birch bark canoes into the Chicago River in 1673, Venice had been at the height of its naval and commercial powers for more than 200 years. Chicago had a lot of catching up to do – and catching up is what it did. Shortly after its incorporation in 1837, Chicago became the fastest growing city in the nation, and during this unparalleled period of expansion and civic awakening, Chicago harbored a crush on Venice.

Chicago was almost totally devastated by the Great Fire in 1871, but Chicagoans – with their indomitable "I will" spirit – regrouped quickly. Little more than 20 years later, Chicago hosted the 1893 World's Columbian Exhibition (World's Fair). Venice was the major inspiration for the design of the "White City," as the fairgrounds were called. Daniel Burnham and the Fair's design team even imported a group of Venetian gondoliers as well as authentic Venetian gondolas, to row visitors for 50 cents a ride on the Fair's Venetian-like canals, reflecting pool and lagoon.

Modeled after a 14TH century Venetian *palazzo*, the Chicago Athletic Association building at 12 South Michigan Avenue, designed by Henry Ives Cobb, was completed in 1893 in time to impress visitors to the Fair. If this *palazzo* were in Venice, you would look down to see its stone tracery reflected in the waters of the Grand Canal. Until recently Chicagoans had to cross Michigan Avenue and look up to appreciate this extraordinary building, but today its striking façade is reflected in the highly polished surface of Anish Kapoor's Cloud Gate sculpture in Chicago's Millennium Park. A few years after the Fair, Chicago also acquired its own version of Venice's Ca' d'Oro. The Gothic stone lacework of the Venice original is echoed in the façade of a residence, still standing today at 1258 North Lake Shore Drive, which was built in 1896 for real estate investor Arthur T. Aldis and his wife Mary.

Chicago looked up to Venice for more than its architecture. Soon after the Fair, Chicago was hailed as the city of the future, not only known for its skyscrapers, but also for the civic aspiration and towering pride they represented. The famous Plan of Chicago, developed by the Commercial Club in 1912, aspired to the ideals embodied in the Acropolis in Athens and the Piazza San Marco in Venice. Today, some people are able to take a break from their work in the sunny landscaped plaza of One Financial Place, dominated by an equestrian statue, standing in a fountain and pool. Entitled *San Marco II*, this sculpture, cast in Venice by Ludovico de Luigi, a fifth-generation Venetian artist, was modeled on the renowned horses that overlook the Piazza San Marco from the Basilica. In fact, just before its voyage to Chicago, de Luigi's horse proudly floated down the Grand Canal in Venice on a barge, complete with a flowing-tressed Venetian woman riding upon its back.

There is still much for us to learn from Venice. While location is critical to a city's growth, it doesn't necessarily guarantee longevity. History points to many examples of places with natural advantages that did not stand the test of time. It is something else that makes cities like Venice and Chicago thrive – a venturesome spirit, openness to new ideas, and even, perhaps, a rugged indifference to challenging weather – the increasingly frequent incidence of high water in Venice, and the icy wind and snow that signal winter in Chicago.

Midway between the West and the East, Venice constantly took advantage of new discoveries from all directions. In re-imagining our city after the Great Fire, Chicagoans took advantage of *new* means of building design and construction and created the world's first skyscraper and, thus, made the modern city possible. These innovations included the metal skeleton frame, the elevator (of course), air conditioning and the type of caisson construction devised by Adler and Sullivan for the Auditorium Theatre in 1894, soon the norm for tall buildings everywhere. Today Chicago presents the world with a *new* model for public spaces – Millennium Park. Like the Piazza San Marco in the 15TH century, Millennium Park in the 21ST century anticipates what people will expect of public places in the future and what other forward-thinking cities will emulate for centuries to come.

In becoming a modern city, Chicago also became a city of reflections, like Venice. Although Chicago's streets are paved with asphalt, not luminous water, our skyscrapers are clad in reflective glass and stone. They capture and refract light in a way that is as identifiable with Chicago as is the glimmer of canal water reflected on a ceiling in Venice. We call this phenomenon "the Chicago effect." Sunlight bounces off skyscrapers to brighten sidewalks below, even those normally in shadow, and can illuminate north-facing offices enough to keep plants flourishing. Moreover, sunrises and sunsets make the façades of our high-rises glow and radiate ever-changing light and color. Rays of setting sunlight are reflected in a west-facing building and then are mirrored in the windows of a building facing east. At dawn, this spectacular exchange of reflections is reversed. Because this lovely occurrence makes us wonder which is the sunlight and which is the reflection, it is akin to what is called "the Venice effect" – the way that Venice blurs the boundary between reality and art.

Venice's canals give back the light and our gaze is drawn down to a second city shimmering on the surface of rippling water. With the wake of a passing boat, the toss of a coin from a bridge or the softest breeze, the reflection of a *palazzo* changes shape, breaks up into an undulant mosaic of colors, and reconstitutes as a *palazzo* again when the water stills – but never the same one twice. In Venice, there is a unique interplay among buildings and nature, water, light and color that is impossible to describe. To understand this Venice, the one that Peter lives with every winter and the city so many of us return to whenever we can, you need only to spend time with his amazing photographs in this book.

Robert A. Wislow
Chairman and CEO, U.S. Equities Realty

14 *L'ucello*

The Fabric of Light

I can no longer remember what it was like not to love Venice. I arrived for my first visit six years ago in early November. A water taxi met me at Marco Polo airport just as the sun was setting. After half an hour on dark lagoon water, reflecting neither moon nor stars that night, we eventually entered the Grand Canal, glided under the Rialto Bridge, and finally arrived at the dock at Santa Maria del Giglio where the landlord of the apartment I was renting met me. I followed him through a very narrow street into a brightly lit *campo* (square), over a *ponte* (bridge), into a small courtyard, and up a flight of stairs into my apartment. Though I had pored over a very detailed map before I arrived, I didn't really know where I was – yet. Of course, I was in a labyrinth called Venice.

The Magician of Venice

I set out the next morning to find the Palazzo Pesaro, now the Museo Fortuny. Once it had been the home and studio of fabric designer Mariano Fortuny y Madrazo (1871–1949). In an exhibit of his work, I naturally expected to see costumes inspired by ancient Greece, the Far East and the Renaissance, made of sumptuous velvets along with the innovative pleated silk he patented that became his signature. His creations were coveted by Isadora Duncan, Sarah Bernhardt and Peggy Guggenheim, as well as fictional characters. In his *Remembrance of Things Past*, Marcel Proust refers to Fortuny at least a dozen times. It is clear that Proust thought Fortuny's work was both inspired by and synonymous with the interplay of light, color and water that makes Venice so enchanting. He describes a particular Fortuny fabric worn by one of his characters as "being of an intense blue which…was changed into malleable gold" by the light, just as the light "changes the azure of the Grand Canal into flaming metal."

Proust's descriptions may be over the top, but to be fair, nothing in Venice is ever in *plain* sight. Sometimes the water does look like blue and gold enameling or like shot silk that changes color with the angle of the light. In November, the very air around San Giorgio Maggiore does turn pink and silver in the dawn when viewed from the dining room of the Hotel Danieli. The undersides of balconies in *palazzi* (palaces) along the canal are encrusted with carvings because they might be viewed from the water, illuminated by reflected light. Eventually, it seems perfectly understandable that Venice is frequently referred to as a stage set. The *palazzi* facing the Grand Canal have beautiful façades, but their land entrances are often inconspicuous. Always lit for dramatic effect, Venice is meant to be seen mainly from the water.

The exhibit I saw had very few Fortuny gowns or fabrics, but I learned why Fortuny was called the magician of Venice. He was a nonpareil – a stage-set designer, painter, photographer, lighting technician, furniture maker and inventor, as well as a dress and fabric designer. He had many gifts, all easily attributed to his living in this watery city, bathed in mutable light. They were an impresario's sense of stage beauty, a painter's interest in color and a physicist's curiosity about optics, which may be, in the end, the most Venetian of these talents.

Fortuny was one of the first people to embrace the dramatic possibilities that electricity presented for the theater. He patented many stage and lighting innovations, including the dimmer switch. As the story goes, Fortuny developed his indirect lighting technique by observing rays of sunlight piercing a darkened room in his *palazzo*. These rays even have a name in Italian – *sciobalati*, or daggers. He concluded in *Éclairage Scénique* (1904) that "if the light were shone onto a surface which was multi-colored, and which could be moved up to or away from the light source, the reflected light would take on the same colors and also be controllable in its intensity." Based on this observation, his invention, the cyclorama dome, can give depth to and change stage lighting from the bright sunlight of a scene painted by Francesco Guardi, for example, to the pearly dusk of J.M.W. Turner or the wintry grey of Antonio Canaletto. Fortuny's reflector lamp works on the same principle and, today, is widely used off stage. In fact, one of these lamps is part of the décor in the lobby bar of the Hard Rock Hotel in Chicago.

Glass Like Water

This passion for seeing has a long history in Venice. Venetians live in a city surrounded by water that is shallow, clear and often reflective as a mirror. They also live with the knowledge that glass, like water, bends light and can alter color. So it is not surprising that Venetians have made many contributions to the study of optics. For example, it took human beings a long time to understand the actual workings of the eye. The ancients thought at first that eyes *produced* light, which bounced off objects, making them visible. Eventually, the Arab mathematician Al-azen (d. 1038) suggested that eyes *receive* light. However, it was a Venetian, Father Paolo Sarpi (d. 1623), known best for his religious treatises, who discovered that the iris opens and closes in relationship to the amount of light it receives.

In addition to his work on the iris, Father Sarpi also is known for bringing Galileo to Venice in 1609 to demonstrate the telescope. Contrary to popular belief, Galileo did not invent the telescope, but he did improve it by creating lenses with high magnification. Thus, he could show the Doge of Venice (from Latin *dux*; Italian *duce* or duke) that approaching ships could be sighted two hours before they arrived. When Galileo turned his telescope to the sky, however, he got into trouble with the church. Galileo discovered, contrary to the then-prevailing view, that the earth was not the only planet with an orbiting moon, which led him, in turn, to agree with Copernicus that the universe was not geocentric.

An invention like the telescope was not possible until people understood how light was bent by glass and until glass could be made as transparent as clear water – a crucial Venetian contribution. A city married to the sea had all the elements for making glass – sand, the ashes of burned vegetation and lime, but there is art, if not alchemy in the process. Venice dominated the glass industry from the 13TH to the 17TH centuries. During the Renaissance, Venetian glassmakers were especially renowned because of their work with a lightweight, transparent glass, called *cristallo*. A Muranese glassmaker, Angelo Barovier, was credited with inventing it in 1450. *Cristallo* re-creates the qualities of rock crystal, but without the weight. Rock crystal had been used to make the clunky hand-held magifiers called reading stones. I like to imagine that a Venetian, perhaps a middle-aged glassblower on Murano, invented spectacles.

Adapters more than innovators, Venetians did not invent mirrors, which had been made from highly polished metals since Greek and Roman times. However, Venetians were the first to create glass mirrors, renowned for their clarity, by backing glass with a thin leaf of metal. Thus, in the Renaissance,

Venice earned the monopoly for these luxury items. So important was their glass art, that punishment was severe for those Venetians who shared the secret of this craft beyond the city. In 1700, Venice also became known for its curvaceous, mouth-blown glass chandeliers, lauded for bravura of design and the unsurpassed ability of her artists to charm glass into the graceful forms of flowers or bunches of grapes, which reflected candlelight in the evening, and sunlight during the day.

In technique especially, Venetian glassmakers remain peerless to this day. The American studio glass master, Dale Chihuly (b. 1941), sought early in his career to apprentice to the master glassmakers in Venice to "absorb the magic of Venetian teamwork and technical wizardry built up over seven hundred years." Chihuly's "Laguna Murano Chandelier," created in collaboration with two Italian glass masters, Lino Tagliapietra and Pino Signoretto, is a tour de force. Part of the chandelier hangs from the ceiling and the other portion erupts from the floor. Both bundles of curling glass are playfully adorned with scallops, sharks and other sea creatures. It takes someone who works with glass to really see the water in its origins. Chihuly has said: "Glass is so much like water. If you let it go on its own, it almost ends up looking like something that came from the sea."

A Floating World

In trying to understand Venice, it is important to consider what it means to live in a floating world. A cluster of 118 small islands, Venice is crisscrossed by 100 canals, connected by 400 bridges, and set in a shallow lagoon where the average depth is 20 inches, a navigational challenge. The lagoon teems with aquatic life, providing many Venetians with a livelihood. The large island of Sant'Erasmo, for example, still produces much of the fruit and vegetables consumed in Venice.

From the air, the dappled color of the water signals the variable depths of the lagoon. Its waters are dotted with islands large and small, alongside numerous *barene* (islets) that are fully submerged only when the tides rise to their highest level. A small island might provide a place for a family to have a picnic outing, if the rower can read the tides and currents of the lagoon. A less practiced rower might ground his boat on a muddy *barene*, visible only at low tide – if he drifts beyond the well-marked and, in many cases, greatly deepened navigation channels.

Rivers pour into the lagoon. In fact, by the 16TH century they had to be diverted so as not to deposit silt in the canals. Waters now move freely through Venice. The canals are refreshed with the incoming and outgoing ocean tides. However when high tide, rising winds and variances in atmospheric pressure combine, Venice can become flooded with *acqua alta* (high water). Many people are working to find a way to protect the city from increasingly severe flooding and to preserve the fragile ecosystem of the lagoon.

For Paolo Barbaro, a native returning after many years away, the omnipresence of water means that Venetians still live in close relation to nature. "…here the canals and *rii* (small canals), the lost islands and ancient rivers, the sandbanks and muddy bottoms, the flora and fauna, the crabs and the flowers, the voices crying out over the waters, the embankments and boats, the *fondamente* and *vere da pozzo* (wellheads), the ebb and flow of the sea – all this continues to be an integral, lived-in part of the city, under our very houses, *inside* our very houses."

Liquid Light and Sound

Because Venetians live with the city's watery beauty, its diffused and reflected light also becomes as much a part of the environment as the water itself. Architects take conscious advantage of this liquid light. Andrea Palladio certainly did. The ceilings of his Venetian churches, especially Il Redentore on Giudecca, are illuminated by light reflected from the water outside. Moreover, when you read about the flicker of seawater playing on the ceiling of the palace in a Henry James novel, you know the setting is Venice. According to Erica Jong, this "shimmer of canal water on a ceiling is so unique to this city that there is a phrase for it in the Venetian dialect, *fa la vecia*, which, translated literally means 'to do as the old woman does' or, idiomatically, 'to squint.'" Count Girolamo Marcello calls this "the Venice effect" in John Berendt's *The City of Falling Angels*: "Sunlight on a canal is reflected up through a window onto the ceiling, then from the ceiling onto a vase, and from the vase onto a glass, or a silver bowl. Which is the real sunlight? Which is the real reflection?"

Venice appeals primarily to the eye and dares artists to capture her opalescent surfaces, which constantly change with shifting light and drifting fog. As a result, Venetians have just as many words for fog – *nebbia, nebbietta, foschia, caligo* – as the Eskimos have for snow. Form disappears in this protean light, and those who render her luminosity best must be masters of color. Venetian paintings, especially in the Renaissance, have long been admired for the way they capture and reflect light, causing generations of art historians to wonder how their bright, intense colors were created. Objects and figures often appear to glow from within. For his mastery, the Venetian painter Veronese, for example, had been called "The Magician of Color." When you think about the pervasiveness of the glass industry in Venice at its height, the conclusion is not surprising. Recently, a conservation scientist re-examined microscopic paint samples from a handful of Venetian paintings she had been studying. She found the same glass particles routinely used by Venetian glassmakers to create *cristallo* actually mixed in the Venetian paints.

Through the alchemy of water, however, visual and aural effects combine to create other experiences unique to Venice. While a visitor may be amazed by the sight of "streets filled with water," the sounds that carry over these waterways often leave a more lasting impression. In the absence of familiar noises, you are able to hear your own *passi* (footsteps) echoing off the water of the canals, as you walk at night, moving from one pool of light to another, through various *campi* and over *ponti*. You may hear the voice of the popular Italian singer, Laura Pausini, wafting over the canal from an apartment down the way. You hear bells ringing from one or another of the city's 100 *campanili* (bell towers) during the day into evening. Later, when you listen to the slower movements of music composed in Venice – by Antonio Vivaldi or Baldassare Galuppi, for starters – you may remember the first time you heard the water lapping gently against the sides of a canal.

A Clouded Mirror

Some of today's visitors may have first encountered Venice in the watercolors of Turner or in the oil paintings of Canaletto and Guardi, which hang in major museums outside of Venice. In many cases, these painted *vedute* (views) served as the postcards of their day. In fact, wealthy young men who made Venice an important port of call on their Grand Tour of Europe in the 18th century often returned home with a canvas or two. This genteel form of leisure travel was to be succeeded by mass tourism. In 1867, for example, Thomas Cook offered his first tour of Venice. By the end of the 19TH century, there already were too many tourists for Henry James. Moreover, he concluded that "originality of attitude" was impossible, especially for those who wanted to be left alone in Venice to make discoveries on their own. Tourism continues to increase.

On Black Sunday, May 3, 1987, 150,000 tourists-for-a-day overwhelmed Venice – a city the size of New York's Central Park. For them, this day would be about choices: taking a *vaporetto* ride down the Grand Canal or a quick tour through the Basilica of San Marco or the Ducal Palace; having a long lunch or seeing a few important paintings at the Accademia art gallery; stopping for a *cappuccino* at Florian's, a Bellini at Harry's Bar or doing a little shopping at Rialto. A day is never enough to know Venice, even for the poet Mario Stefani, who was very welcoming to visitors: "Anyone who loves Venice is a true Venetian, even a tourist, but only if the tourist stays long enough to appreciate the city. If he stays only one day just to say he's been to Venice, no."

In a city which has revived itself commercially through tourism, the republic's brilliant history may be past, yet it is not absent. But there is no need to commit its details to memory before arriving. The arc of its story is simple and familiar: triumph and loss, accommodation and renewal. This story begins as an epic. Venice was founded in the year 421 on March 24. Romans in the Veneto, fleeing from the Goths, sought refuge in the chain of 118 islands in the shallow lagoon. Bridging the east and west, Venice prospers, becoming a naval and a commercial power. This is Venice at high tide. It develops a working, if not a consistently model republic. Interestingly, the Doge was chosen by lot. Until the end of the 18TH century, Venice holds sway over an empire, which encompassed the Adriatic and stretched to Constantinople. Then its fortunes begin to ebb; and the city is in low tide.

Venice is defeated in 1797 by Napoleon, who robbed Venice of many of its treasures, including the famous horse sculptures of San Marco that La Serenissima had originally plundered from Constantinople. They were eventually returned to Venice, but with their ruby eyes missing. In one of the most moving accounts of this end of the Republic, John Julius Norwich wrote that on May 12, 1797, Ludovico Manin, last Doge of Venice, took off his *corno*, the peculiarly-shaped hat that signified this position, "untied the ribbons of the close-fitting cap of white linen worn beneath it, the *cuffetta*, and handed it to his valet, saying: 'Take it, I shall not be needing it again' (*Tolè questa no la dopero più*)."

In its years of occupation, Venice is in dry water, its treasuries emptying. Austrian rule follows Napoleon's; French rule briefly returns and is followed again by Austrian occupation. In 1848 under the leadership of Daniele Manin, Venice regains independence for little more than a year. Once the Queen of the Adriatic, Venice is folded into a unified Italy in 1866, and her waters are still, poised between movements.

Here the story continues as a romance, tinged with the melancholy so appealing to generations of visitors. So think again about Venetian mirrors. In the prime of the Venetian republic, her mirrors were commercially valued for their splendid clarity. After her fall, one romantic storyteller after another lovingly repeats the image of a clouded mirror, hanging in a dark *palazzo*, reflecting the fading fortunes of a once great family. This wistfulness for the past has become synonymous with Venice. But the Venetian glass industry, nearly destroyed when Venice was occupied, was revived in the mid-19TH century. Glassmakers recovered the old forms and began producing the drinking glasses, chandeliers and mirrors which appealed to tourists then and still do today. Unforgettably, it is a Venetian red glass goblet that draws Katharine Hepburn into the shop in Campo San Barnaba where she meets Rossano Brazzi in that valentine of a film to Venice, David Lean's *Summertime*.

Waters of the Imagination

Some Venetians describe themselves with a nautical term, *andare all a deriva*, meaning 'to be adrift,' perhaps in time. Today, it is a rare *palazzo* that has been continuously occupied by the family for whom it was built. Fewer and fewer current residents, perhaps less than a third, can count a Venetian great grandfather in their family tree. Yet their ancestors did create a city out of nothing more than water, sand and the glass that is made from it. They created a city which has become almost mythical in importance, like Alexandria or Byzantium. True, the central core of the city has been losing population and the movement of water against the buildings is taking its toll. But it is an ancient city that has been continuously inhabited since its founding. There is still a Venetian saying about the birth of a native child: "A lord is born." Understandably, Venice's children are still heirs to the idea of the great republic.

Many people wonder, "Is Venice dying?" Before looking for an answer, it is important to consider how difficult it is to get at the truth in Venice. For example, there is a Venetian proverb: "To know the truth you must listen to two liars (*Par saver £a verità, bexogna sentir do buxiari*)." Therefore, a Venetian, comfortable with the nebulous border between sea and sky, between the real sunlight and reflection, might very well answer "Which Venice?" Venetians have always lived with at least two of them – the Venice they built on a crescent of marshy islands and the one fabricated by light in the surrounding waters. Both are real to them. Guido Brunetti, the Commissario of Police in the latest of Donna Leon's novels set in Venice, has time to think one morning about the mirrored waters of the Grand Canal, while waiting for the police launch: "He looked on what his ancestors had seen: the same light, the same façades, the same windows and plants, and the same vital silence. And, as far as he could distinguish the reflections, it all existed double."

Successive waves of artists, writers and just ordinary lovers of Venice have tried to describe the enigmatic appeal this city has for them. In the end, Venice is a place that can really only be experienced, not explained. On my first visit, I had thought that a month would be more than enough time to become acquainted with Venice. But the longer I stayed and the more frequently I returned, I discovered that Venice reveals its general contours to everyone, rewards those who come back to its ever-changing iridescent surfaces, but keeps those who truly love the city – even its natives – always looking for something more beyond the crowded streets, the museums and architectural wonders. There really is only one place to look, and it has been there all along. Novelist Jeanette Winterson has said it well: "The only way to get at Venice is to use the water – its refractions, reflections, the play of light and shadow, and to re-create Venice where it has always been strongest – in the imagination."

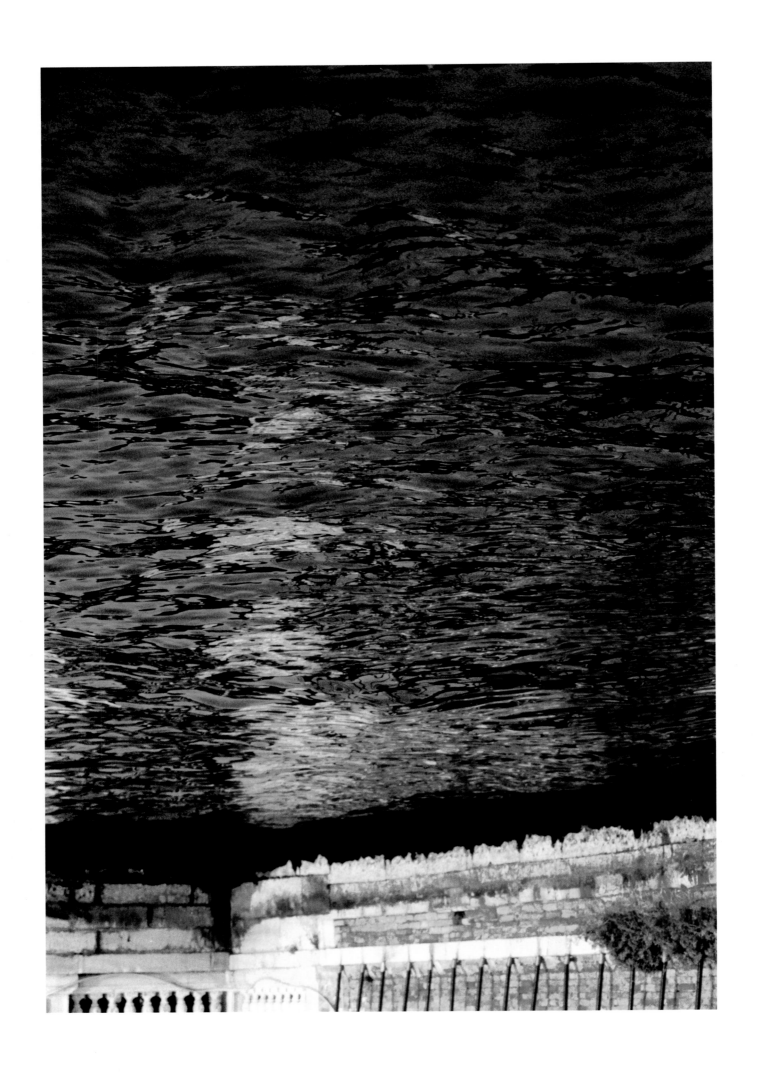

Reflections — Riflessioni

Italy has many languages – one of them is Venetian, established long ago in the loneliness of the lagoon in which Venice sits. At the height of Venice's power, this was the language of princes, conquerors and traders. Now it is a familial dialect separating Venetians from others.

> **L'Italia ha molte lingue** – una di esse è il veneziano – stabilitosi molto tempo fa nella solitudine della laguna in cui Venezia è assisa. All'apice del potere della Repubblica di Venezia, questa era la lingua dei prìncipi, dei conquistatori e dei commercianti. Ora è il linguaggio famigliare che distingue i veneziani dagli altri.

Proverbio Veneziano – Remo curto, barca piccola.   **Venetian proverb** – Short oar, small boat.

Ombra **is an Italian word.** It means shadow. In Venice – and only in Venice – it also means a glass of wine (red or white). And that is because by the end of the 19TH century the *cittadini* (citizens) were taking their afternoon glass of wine well protected from the searing summer sun on Piazza San Marco in the *ombra* of great canopies strung from the Campanile or the arcades.

> **Ombra è una parola italiana.** A Venezia – e solo a Venezia – significa anche un bicchiere di vino (rosso o bianco). Ciò è dovuto al fatto che, un tempo, i suoi "cittadini" si bevevano il loro bicchiere pomeridiano di vino, ben protetti dal sole cocente di Piazza San Marco "all'ombra" di grandi tendoni stesi vicino al Campanile e ai portici.

Gabriele D'Annunzio (1863–1938) – *Il Fuoco*
Descrivendo il chiostro di Santa Apollonia a Venezia:
…un piccolo chiostro segreto, aperto su un ordine di colonne assottigliate e accoppiate come le monache quando passeggiano digiune al sole, delicatissime, non bianche, non grigie, non nere ma del più misterioso colore che mai abbia dato alla pietra quel gran maestro colorista che si chiama il Tempo.

> Describing the cloister of Santa Apollonia in Venice:
> *…a small hidden cloister, opening to a row of narrow double columns that look like a march of fasting nuns walking in the sun – extremely delicate, not white, not gray, not black but the most mysterious color ever given to stone by the greatest colorist of all – Father Time.*

Peggy Guggenheim (1898–1979) – *A Life Dedicated to Art. Confessions of a woman who loved art and artists.*
…It has always been taken for granted that Venice is the ideal city for a honeymoon, but that is a big mistake. To live in Venice…means that you fall in love with her and no room remains in your heart for anything else. The same goes for the Venetians…their love grows with the rising tide and diminishes with the ebb tide.

> *…Si è sempre dato per scontato che Venezia sia la città ideale per una luna di miele, ma è un grave errore. Vivere a Venezia… significa innamorarsene cosi che nel cuore non resta più posto per altro. Così è anche per i veneziani… il loro amore cresce con la marea che sale e si attenua con la marea calante.*

Robert Benchley (1889–1945)
Telegram from Venice to his editor: *Streets flooded. Please advise.*

> Telegramma da Venezia al suo editore: *Strade allagate. Datemi istruzioni.*

Giorgio Bassani (1916–2000) – *Il Giardino dei Finzi-Contini*
…Era stato a Venezia, proseguì, forse per suggestione delle nebbie locali che erano così diverse dai nostri cupi nebbioni padani, nebbie infinitamente più luminose e vaghe (soltanto un pittore al mondo aveva saputo renderle: più che il tardo Monet, il nostro De Pisis…)

> *…he had been to Venice, he went on, maybe because of the magic of the fog there, so different from our dark, heavy fog of the Po valley, a fog immensely more luminous and pretty (only one painter in the world has been able to recreate it: better than the late Monet our own De Pisis…)*

Claude Monet (1840–1929)
Everyone discusses my art and pretends to understand it, as if it were necessary to understand. It is simply necessary to love.

> *Tutti discutono della mia arte e fingono di capirla, come se ce ne fosse bisogno, quando sarebbe semplicemente necessario amarla.*

***Arsenale* is a Venetian word.** It comes from the Arabic "Arzana" or "dar-as-sina-ah," which means shipyard – and the walled shipyard in Venice, *l'Arsenale*, takes up a big chunk of the city's real estate.

When Venice ruled the world it was because of the power of its navy and the navy's ability to be supplied by its *Arsenale* – so in English the word "arsenal" has come to mean a protected cache of weapons. The *Arsenale* is now home to the Biennale's cache of installation art.

> **Arsenale è una parola veneziana.** Deriva dall'arabo – "Arzana" o "dar-as-sina-ah" – che significa "cantiere navale" – e il cantiere fortificato navale di Venezia, l'Arsenale, occupa un bel pezzo della superficie della città.
>
> Quando Venezia dominava il mondo, ciò era dovuto alla potenza della sua marina militare e anche alla possibilità che la stessa aveva di approvigionarsi al suo Arsenale – così che la parola inglese "arsenal" ha preso il significato di un deposito di armamenti vari. L'Arsenale è ora divenuto la residenza di quel "deposito" di installazioni artistiche che è la Biennale.

Dante Alighieri (1265–1321) – *Divina Commedia*, canto XXI° – *L'Inferno*
…Quale nell'arzana de viniziani bolle l'inverno la tenace pece a rimpalmar li legni lor non sani, che navigar non ponno; e'n quella vece chi fa suo legno nuovo, e chi ristoppo le coste a quel che più viaggi fece; chi ribatte da prora, e chi da poppa, altri fa remi, ed altri volge sarte chi terzeruolo, ed artimon rintoppa…

> *…(it is) such as the Venetians' arsenal in winter, where the viscous pitch is boiling to restore the damaged ships that cannot sail; where some make their own new boats, some fix the wood of those that are most travel weary, some hammer the bows, some the sterns, others make oars and others tend to the sails and fix the rudders…*

Proverbio Veneziano
L'ombra de l'istà fa mal a la panza d'inverno.

Venetian proverb
The shadow of summer doesn't bode well for the belly of winter.

Robert Browning (1812–1889)
An entablature on the Rio S. Barnaba side of Ca' Rezzonico:
Robert Browning died in this palazzo on December 11, 1889 – "open my heart and you will see graved inside of it Italy."

> Una tavoletta sul lato Rio S. Barnaba di Ca' Rezzonico:
> *Robert Browning morì in questo palazzo l'11 dicembre 1889 – "aprite il mio cuore e ci vedrete inciso Italia."*

A gondola is a Venetian canoe-like boat. One of many particular crafts that ply the canals of Venice, it is manned by a single oarsman who rests his oar against a vertical fulcrum of wood at the back right side of the boat called a *forcola*. The gondola is built (bent to the right) like a banana (look carefully next time). This counteracts the push of the oar to the left. The boats are black and are of a size – by old law – after several centuries of outlandish colorful competition – causing no end of fender bending in the canals.

> **Una gondola è un'imbarcazione veneziana simile a una canoa.** Una della molte imbarcazioni che solcano i canali di Venezia, il suo equipaggio è rappresentato da un solo rematore che tiene il suo remo posato su un fulcro verticale di legno, sul lato destro posteriore della imbarcazione, chiamato "forcola". La gondola è costruita con una curva a destra, come una banana (guardatela attentamente la prossima volta). Si contrappone così alla spinta del remo che va a sinistra. Le gondole sembrano essere tutte nere e delle stesse dimensioni – per un antica legge – dopo molti secoli di stravaganti e colorite competizioni – causando così un'infinità di piccoli scontri nei canali.

Erica Jong (1942–)
It is the city of mirrors, the city of mirages, at once solid and liquid, at once air and stone.

> *È la città degli specchi, la città dei miraggi, solida e liquida, acqua e pietra allo stesso tempo.*

Proverbio Veneziano
Detto per deridere chi a tavola preferisce bere acqua
piuttosto che buon vino – *(Ma)...l'acqua smarsise i pai!*

Venetian proverb
Said as a joke to someone at table who prefers water
to fine wine – *(But)...water rots posts!*

Note: there are multi-colored pylons encrusted everywhere in the canals of Venice.

Henry James (1843–1916)
Though there are some disagreeable things in Venice there is nothing so disagreeable as the visitors.

Sebbene vi siano certe cose sgradevoli a Venezia, non v'è niente di più sgradevole della gente che la visita.

Mary McCarthy (1912–1989) – *Venice Observed*
...that is how the Allies took Venice, arriving from the mainland, at the end of the Second World War. There was a gasoline shortage, and the Allied command, having made secret contact with the gondoliers' co-operative, officially "captured" Venice with a fleet of gondolas. Even war in Venice evokes a disbelieving smile.

...È così che gli Alleati presero Venezia, arrivando dall'entroterra, verso la fine della Seconda Guerra Mondiale. C'era scarsità di benzina e il Comando Alleato, dopo aver preso contatti segreti con l'associazione dei gondolieri, "catturò" ufficialmente Venezia con una flotta di gondole. A Venezia, perfino la guerra puo' far nascere un sorriso di incredulità.

Snob is an Italian word. It is a contraction of two words, <u>*se*</u>*nza* <u>*nobilità*</u> (or <u>*sine*</u> <u>*nobilitate*</u> – Lat.), which together mean "without nobility" applied by those who (think they) have it to those whom they think don't and who hold their noses higher than they ought.

Snob è una parola Italiana. È la contrazione di due parole, <u>se</u>nza <u>nobilità</u> (o <u>s</u>ine <u>nobilitate</u> – Lat.), che viene affibbiata da coloro che ne sono (o pensano di esserne) in possesso a quelli che essi ritengono ne siano privi e che ti guardano dall'alto in basso più di quanto dovrebbero.

Virginia Woolf (1882–1941)
I'm glad to find that you dislike Venice, because I thought it detestable when we were there, both times – once it might be due to insanity but not twice, so I thought it must be my fault. I suppose the obscurer reaches might be beautiful.

Sono contenta che non ti piaccia Venezia, perché mi è rimasta odiosa tutt'e due le volte che eravamo lì – la prima volta lo si potrebbe attribuire a pazzia ma non la seconda, così ho pensato che fosse colpa mia. Suppongo che le mète più oscure siano bellissime.

Ciao is a Venetian word. It is used throughout the world to informally say *buon giorno* (good day/hello) or *arrivederci* (goodbye). Its derivation, however, is anything but informal.

Schiavo (ref: Slavonic peoples) means slave in Venetian. The embankment starting at the Doge's palace and running to the Giardini is called *Riva degli Schiavoni* – the Street of Slaves (they worked the docks). So politeness in greeting nobles required:

Schiavo suo or *S' ciavo suo* – I am your slave (servant)

which later shortened to *s'ciavo*

which later shortened to *ciao*

So...*Ciao!* – and enjoy the pictures.

Ciao è una parola veneziana. È usata in tutto il mondo per dire, in tono informale, sia "buongiorno" che "arrivederci". La sua origine, tuttavia, è tutt'altro che informale.

L'argine che ha inizio dal Palazzo Ducale e va fino ai Giardini è chiamato Riva degli Schiavoni, la via degli schiavi (il riferimento è a popolazioni slave), che erano quelli che lavoravano sui moli. Così la cortesia usata nel salutare le persone di nobile famiglia richiedeva le parole:

"Schiavo suo" o "S'ciavo suo"

più tardi accorciato in "S'ciavo"

che poi diventerà "Ciao"

Allora...Ciao! – e godetevi le immagini.

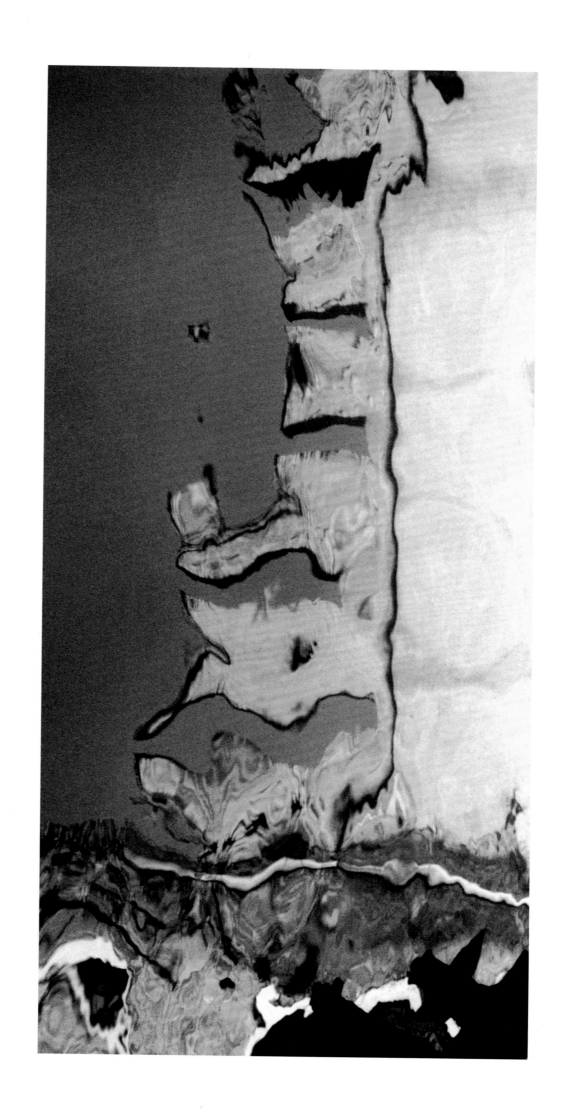

48 *Senza titolo*

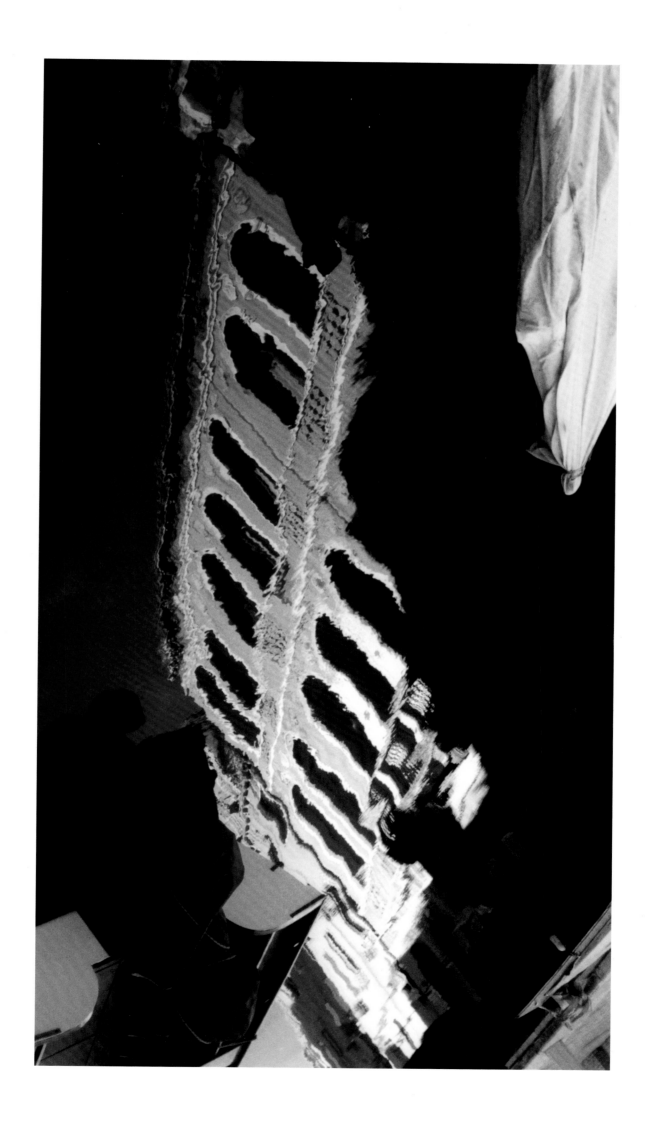

62 *Senza titolo*

64 *Senza titolo*

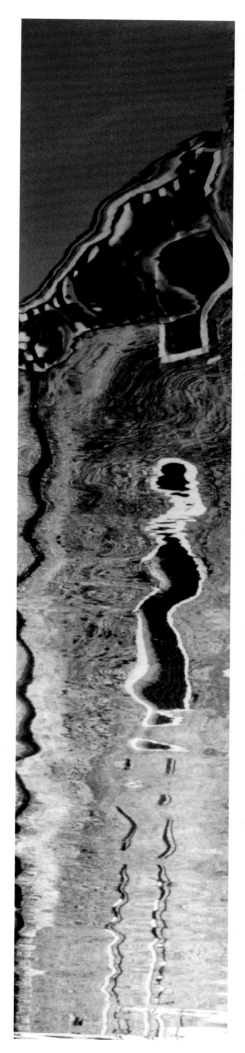
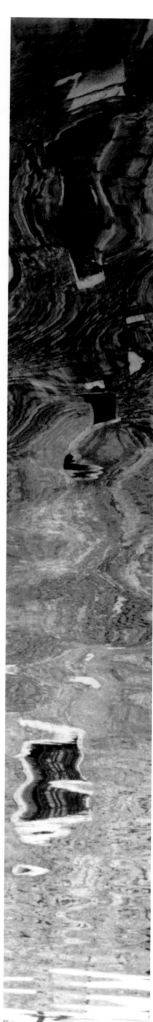

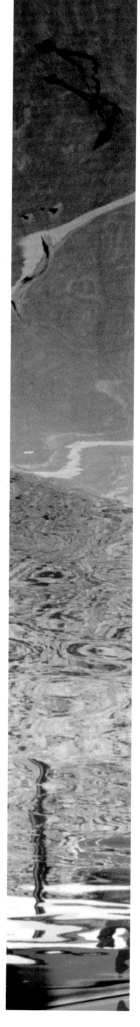

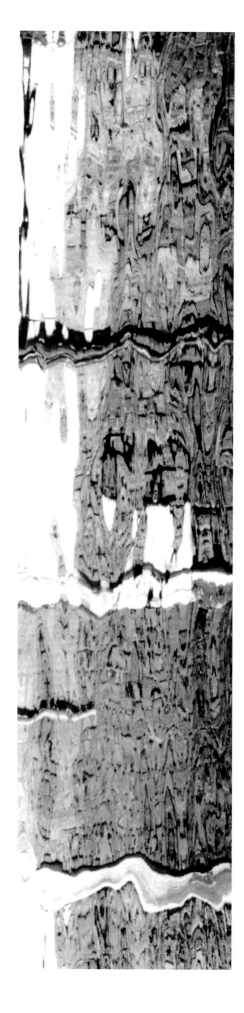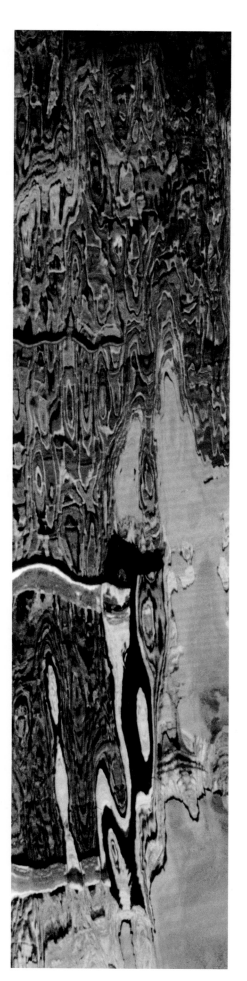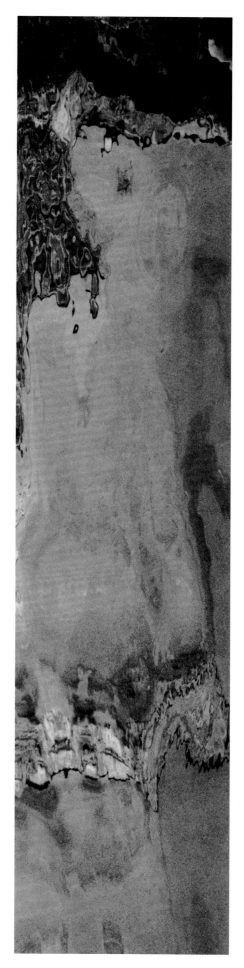

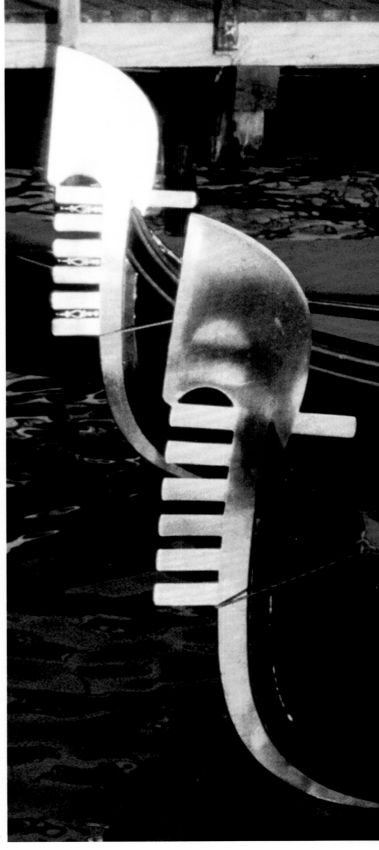

88 *Barriera rossa*

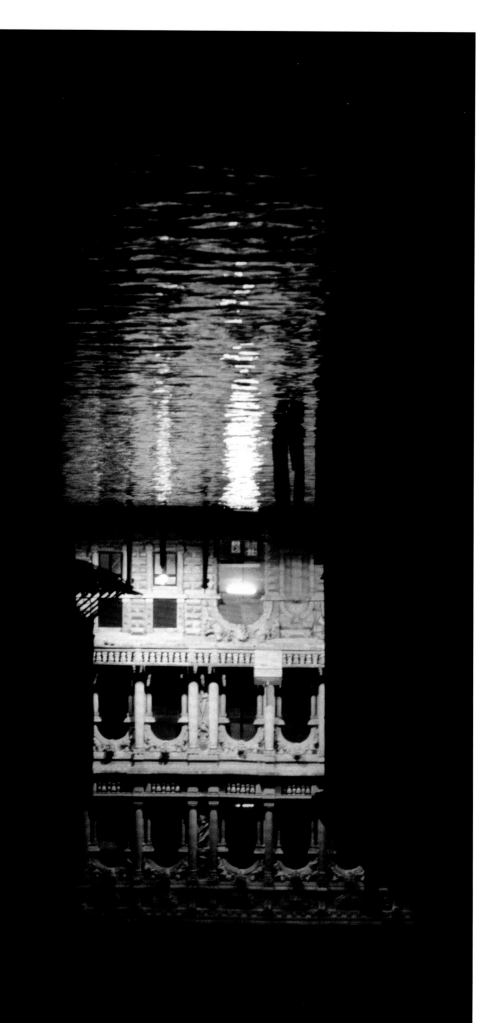

Bibliography

Alighieri, Dante. *Divina Commedia,* canto XXI°.

Barbaro, Paolo. *Venice Revealed. An Intimate Portrait.* Translated by Tami Calliope. South Royalton, Vt: Steerforth Italian, 2001.

Bassani, Giorgio. *Il Giardino dei Finzi-Contini.* Milano: Mondadori, 1986.

Benchley, Robert. http://chatna.com/theme/venice.htm

Berendt, John. *The City of Falling Angels.* New York: The Penguin Press, 2005.

Bonfante-Warren, Alexandra. *Venice.* New York: Barnes & Noble Books, 2000.

Browning, Robert . Entablature at Ca' Rezzonico. Words taken from Browning's poem, "De Gustibus," in *Men and Women,* 1855.

Calcagno, Anne, ed. *Traveler's Tales Italy.* Introduction by Jan Morris. San Francisco: Traveler's Tales, Inc., 2001.

Calvino, Italo. *Invisible Cities.* Translated by William Weaver. New York: Harcourt Brace Jovanovich, 1972.

Crouzet-Pavan, Elisabeth. *Venice Triumphant. The Horizon of a Myth.* Translated by Lydia G. Cochrane. Baltimore & London: The Johns Hopkins University Press, 2002.

D'Annunzio, Gabriele. *Il Fuoco,* in *Tutte le opere di Gabriele D'Annunzio.* Milano: Mondadori, 1978.

"Dale Chihuly: the George R. Stroempfle Collection. 2003-2004." http://www.lakeview-museum.org/pastexhibits/Chihuly.html

Da Mosto, Francesco. *Francesco's Venice. The Dramatic History of the World's Most Beautiful City.* London: BBC Books, 2004.

Garrett, Martin. *Venice. A Cultural and Literary Companion.* Foreword by Michael Dibdin. Northampton and New York: Interlink Books, 2001.

Goho, Alexandra. "Venetian Grinds." *Science on Line.* March 12, 2005.

Guggenheim, Peggy. *A Life Dedicated to Art. Confessions of a woman who loved art and artists.* Preface by Gore Vidal. Milano: Rizzoli, 1998.

Harris, Sandra. *Venice Revisited.* London: Pavilion Books LTD, 2003.

Hawkins, Jennifer Opie, ed. *Chihuly at the V & A.* Seattle: Portland Press, 2001.

Hodgson, Barbara. *Italy Out of Hand. A Capricious Tour.* San Francisco: Chronicle Books, 2005.

Howard, Deborah, Fabrice Moireau, and Trudy Sammartini. *Venice Sketchbook.* New York: St. Martin's Press, 2004.

James, Henry. *Italian Hours*. New York: Penguin Books, 1995.

Jong, Erica. "City of Love and Death: Venice." *New York Times on the web*. March 23, 1986.

Jong, Erica. http://www.corsinet.com/braincandy/qcity.html#Venice

Kassinger, Ruth. "Inventions that Use Light," *Build a Better Mousetrap*. San Francisco: Jossey-Bass, 2002.

Leon, Donna. *Through a Glass Darkly*. New York: Grove/Atlantic, 2006.

Lovric, Michelle. *Venice. Tales of the City*. London: Abacus, 2005.

"Mariano Fortuny: Designer Profile." http://www.lightology.com/index.cfm/method-light. mariano_fortuny.

Marqusee, Michael, ed. *Venice. An Illustrated Anthology*. Introduction by Anthony Burgess. Topsfield, MA: Salem House Publishers, 1989.

McCarthy, Mary. *Venice Observed*. New York: Harcourt Brace & Company, 1963.

Mentzel, Peter. *A Traveller's History of Venice*. Northampton, MA; Interlink Publishing Group, 2006.

Monet, Claude. http://www.humanitiesweb.org

Morris, Jan. *The World of Venice*. Revised Edition. London: Harcourt Brace & Company, 1993.

Norwich, John Julius. *A History of Venice*. New York: Vintage Books, 1989.

--------, ed. *A Traveller's Companion to Venice*. Northampton, MA & New York: Interlink Books, 2002.

Panek, Richard. *Seeing and Believing. How the Telescope Opened Our Eyes and Minds to the Heavens*. New York: Viking, 1998.

Proverbi & Modi di Dire. "I Schéi no i ga ganbe ma i core." Padova: Simonelli Editore, 2005.

Tanner, Tony. *Venice Desired*. Cambridge: Harvard University Press, 1992.

"The Fortuny Gown." http://www.chick.net/proust/fortuny.html

Venice. Knopf Guide. New York: Alfred A. Knopf, Inc., 1993.

Weideger, Paula. *Venetian Dreaming*. New York: Washington Square Press, 2002.

Winterson, Jeanette. "Invisible Cities." *Building Design*. July 2001. http://www.jeanettewinterson.com

Woolf, Virginia. Letter, April 25, 1913, to Vanessa Bell. *The Question of Things Happening*: Letters, vol. 2, ed. Nigel Nicolson (1976).

Zampedri, Michele. "The History of Murano Glass." http://www.doge.it/murano